Super Incredible!

KNOCK-KNOCK JOKES

for Kids

Bob Phillips

EUGENE, OREGON

Cover by The Dugan Design Group, Bloomington, Minnesota

Cover illustration © The Dugan Design Group

SUPER INCREDIBLE KNOCK-KNOCK JOKES FOR KIDS
Copyright © 2007 by Bob Phillips
Published by Harvest House Publishers
Eugene, Oregon 97402

ISBN-13: 978-0-7369-2019-3

Printed in the United States of America

12 13 14 / BP-SK / 10 9 8

Contents

1

Please Come Back Later!

Knock, knock.
Who's there?
Abby.
Abby who?
Abby birthday to you!

★ ★ ★

Knock, knock.
Who's there?
Abbey.
Abbey who?
Abbey, C, D, E, F, G!

★ ★ ★

Knock, knock.
Who's there?
Ach.
Ach who?
Gesundheit!

★ ★ ★

Knock, knock.
Who's there?
Ada.
Ada who?
Ada lot for breakfast.

★ ★ ★

Knock, knock.
Who's there?
Adair.
Adair who?
Adair once but now I'm bald.

★ ★ ★

Knock, knock.
Who's there?
Adolf.
Adolf who?
Adolf ball hit me in the mowf.

★ ★ ★

Knock, knock.
Who's there?
Agatha!
Agatha who?
Agatha sore tooth! It's killing me!

★ ★ ★

Knock, knock.
Who's there?
Ahmed.
Ahmed who?
Ahmed a mistake! I think I'm at the wrong house.

★ ★ ★

Knock, knock.
Who's there?
Aida.
Aida who?
Aida whole box of chocolates and I feel really sick.

★ ★ ★

Knock, knock.
Who's there?
Aitch.
Aitch who?
Bless you.

Knock, knock.
Who's there?
Alaska.
Alaska who?
Alaska no questions. You tella no lies!

★ ★ ★

Knock, knock.
Who's there?
Albee.
Albee who?
Albee back.

★ ★ ★

Knock, knock.
Who's there?
Hey, Alex.
Hey, Alex who?
Hey, Alex the questions around here.

★ ★ ★

Knock, knock.
Who's there?
Alex.
Alex who?
Alexplain later, just let me in.

★ ★ ★

Knock, knock.
Who's there?
Alfie.
Alfie who?
Alfie crying out loud, stop asking!

* * *

Knock, knock.
Who's there?
Alfred.
Alfred who?
Alfred I got the wrong door. Sorry!

* * *

Knock, knock.
Who's there?
Alison.
Alison who?
Alison to the radio!

* * *

Knock, knock.
Who's there?
Alison.
Alison who?
Alison Wonderland.

* * *

Knock, knock.
Who's there?
Althea.
Althea who?
Althea later, alligator.

★ ★ ★

Knock, knock.
Who's there?
Annapolis.
Annapolis who?
Annapolis a juicy fruit.

★ ★ ★

Knock, knock.
Who's there?
Anthem.
Anthem who?
You anthem devil you.

★ ★ ★

Knock, knock.
Who's there?
Armageddon.
Armageddon who?
Armageddon out of here!

★ ★ ★

Knock, knock.
Who's there?
Arthur.
Arthur who?
Arthur any kids who want to come out and play?

★ ★ ★

Knock, knock.
Who's there?
Arthur.
Arthur who?
Arthur any more jelly beans in the jar?

★ ★ ★

Knock, knock.
Who's there?
Arthur.
Arthur who?
Arthur any other questions you have?

★ ★ ★

Knock, knock.
Who's there?
Arthur.
Arthur who?
Arthur mometer says it's 120 degrees!

★ ★ ★

Knock, knock.
Who's there?
Artichoke.
Artichoke who?
Artichokes when they serve meatloaf for lunch.

★ ★ ★

Knock, knock.
Who's there?
Artichokes.
Artichokes who?
Artichokes when he eats too fast.

★ ★ ★

Knock, knock.
Who's there?
Asia.
Asia who?
Asia father home? He owes me money.

★ ★ ★

Knock, knock.
Who's there?
Atlas.
Atlas who?
Atlas it's Friday, and I'm looking forward to the
    weekend.

* * *

Knock, knock.
Who's there?
Augusta.
Augusta who?
Augusta wind is coming.

* * *

Knock, knock.
Who's there?
Aurora.
Aurora who?
Aurora's just come from a big lion!

* * *

Knock, knock.
Who's there?
Avenue.
Avenue who?
Avenue learned my name yet?

* * *

Knock, knock.
Who's there?
Avenue!
Avenue who?
Avenue heard this joke before?

★ ★ ★

Knock, knock.
Who's there?
Avenue.
Avenue who?
Avenue got a doorbell?

★ ★ ★

Knock, knock.
Who's there?
Ax.
Ax who?
Ax nicely, and I might tell you!

2

Answer the Door!

Knock, knock.
Who's there?
Barbara!
Barbara who?
Barbara black sheep, have you any wool?

★ ★ ★

Knock, knock.
Who's there?
Barbie.
Barbie who?
Barbie Q.

★ ★ ★

Knock, knock.
Who's there?
Barry.
Barry who?
Barry happy to meet you.

★ ★ ★

Knock, knock.
Who's there?
Bat.
Bat who?
Bat you'll never guess!

★ ★ ★

Knock, knock.
Who's there?
Beezer.
Beezer who?
Beezer black and yellow and make honey!

★ ★ ★

Knock, knock.
Who's there?
Bella.
Bella who?
Bella no ringa, thatsa why I knocka.

★ ★ ★

Knock, knock.
Who's there?
Ben.
Ben who?
Ben a long time since I've seen you.

★ ★ ★

Knock, knock.
Who's there?
Ben Hur.
Ben Hur who?
Ben Hur an hour–let me in.

★ ★ ★

Knock, knock.
Who's there?
Blur.
Blur who?
Blur! It's cold out here.

★ ★ ★

Knock, knock.
Who's there?
Boo.
Boo who?
Don't cry, sweetie pie.

★ ★ ★

Knock, knock.
Who's there?
Boo.
Boo who?
Don't cry–it's only a knock-knock joke.

★ ★ ★

Knock, knock.
Who's there?
A little boy.
A little boy who?
A little boy who can't reach the doorbell.

★ ★ ★

Knock, knock.
Who's there?
Butcher.
Butcher who?
Butcher arms around me and give me a big hug.

★ ★ ★

Knock, knock.
Who's there?
Butcher.
Butcher who?
Butcher money where your mouth is.

Knock, knock.
Who's there?
Butter.
Butter who?
Butter open the door, or else!

3

Can I Come In?

Knock, knock.
Who's there?
Candy.
Candy who?
Candy cow jump over the moon?

★ ★ ★

Knock, knock.
Who's there?
Canoe.
Canoe who?
Canoe help me take this fish off my line?

★ ★ ★

Knock, knock.
Who's there?
Canoe.
Canoe who?
Canoe help me with my homework?

★ ★ ★

Knock, knock.
Who's there?
Canoe.
Canoe who?
Canoe lend me some money?

★ ★ ★

Knock, knock.
Who's there?
Carmen.
Carmen who?
Carmen get it!

★ ★ ★

Knock, knock.
Who's there?
Carmen.
Carmen who?
Carmen get me out of the middle of this stampede!

Knock, knock.
Who's there?
Carrie.
Carrie who?
Carrie on with what you're doing.

★ ★ ★

Knock, knock.
Who's there?
Cedar.
Cedar who?
Join the Navy, and cedar world.

★ ★ ★

Knock, knock.
Who's there?
Celery.
Celery who?
Celery dance?

★ ★ ★

Knock, knock.
Who's there?
Cello.
Cello who?
Cello there.

★ ★ ★

Knock, knock.
Who's there?
Charlotte.
Charlotte who?
Charlotte of mosquitoes out tonight.

★ ★ ★

Knock, knock.
Who's there?
Cheese.
Cheese who?
Cheese a jolly good fellow.

★ ★ ★

Knock, knock.
Who's there?
Chuck.
Chuck who?
Chuck me the ball and quit asking so many questions.

★ ★ ★

Knock, knock.
Who's there?
Chuck.
Chuck who?
Chuck and see if you recognize me.

★ ★ ★

Knock, knock.
Who's there?
Claire.
Claire who?
Claire the way! I'm coming through.

★ ★ ★

Knock, knock.
Who's there?
Colleen.
Colleen who?
Colleen all cars!

★ ★ ★

Knock, knock.
Who's there?
Collie.
Collie who?
Collie, Miss Molly, I don't know.

★ ★ ★

Knock, knock.
Who's there?
Congo.
Congo who?
Congo on meeting like this.

★ ★ ★

Knock, knock.
Who's there?
Cook.
Cook who?
You're the one who's cuckoo!

★ ★ ★

Knock, knock.
Who's there?
Cows.
Cows who?
No, cows go moo, not who.

★ ★ ★

Knock, knock.
Who's there?
Crypt.
Crypt who?
Crypt up from behind to scare you!

4

No More Visitors!

Knock, knock.
Who's there?
Dakota.
Dakota who?
Dakota fits fine, but the pants are too long.

★ ★ ★

Knock, knock.
Who's there?
Dana.
Dana who?
Dana talk with your mouth full.

★ ★ ★

Knock, knock.
Who's there?
Datsun.
Datsun who?
Datsun old joke!

★ ★ ★

Knock, knock.
Who's there?
Datsun.
Datsun who?
Datsun other lousy joke!

★ ★ ★

Knock, knock.
Who's there?
Dawn.
Dawn who?
Dawn do anything I wouldn't do.

★ ★ ★

Knock, knock.
Who's there?
Deluxe.
Deluxe who?
Deluxe Ness Monster.

★ ★ ★

Knock, knock.
Who's there?
Denis.
Denis who?
Denis anyone?

★ ★ ★

Knock, knock.
Who's there?
Detail.
Detail who?
Detail is wagging the dog.

★ ★ ★

Knock, knock.
Who's there?
Dewey.
Dewey who?
Dewey have to listen to any more knock-knock jokes?

★ ★ ★

Knock, knock.
Who's there?
Dewey.
Dewey who?
Dewey have any homework tonight?

★ ★ ★

Knock, knock.
Who's there?
Dewey.
Dewey who?
Dewey have to stand outside?

★ ★ ★

Knock, knock.
Who's there?
Dill.
Dill who?
Dill we meet again, my sweet!

★ ★ ★

Knock, knock.
Who's there?
Diploma.
Diploma who?
Diploma to fix da leak.

★ ★ ★

Knock, knock.
Who's there?
Disaster.
Disaster who?
Disaster be my lucky day.

★ ★ ★

Knock, knock.
Who's there?
Disguise.
Disguise who?
Disguise killing me with this knock-knock joke!

★ ★ ★

Knock, knock.
Who's there?
Dishes.
Dishes who?
Dishes the end of the world. Goodbye to all!

★ ★ ★

Knock, knock.
Who's there?
Dishes.
Dishes who?
Dishes a very bad joke!

★ ★ ★

Knock, knock.
Who's there?
Dishes.
Dishes who?
Dishes the way I talk now that I've got falsh teeth.

★ ★ ★

Knock, knock.
Who's there?
Don.
Don who?
Don tell me you don't remember me!

★ ★ ★

Knock, knock.
Who's there?
Donut.
Donut who?
Donut come near me–I'm sneezing.

★ ★ ★

Knock, knock.
Who's there?
Doughnut.
Doughnut who?
Doughnut forsake me, oh my darling.

Knock, knock.
Who's there?
Dozen.
Dozen who?
Dozen anyone answer the door?

★ ★ ★

31

Knock, knock.
Who's there?
Dozen.
Dozen who?
Dozen anyone know my name?

★ ★ ★

Knock, knock.
Who's there?
Dragon.
Dragon who?
Dragon your feet will only make Dad angry.

★ ★ ★

Knock, knock.
Who's there?
Dummy.
Dummy who?
Dummy a favor and get lost.

★ ★ ★

Knock, knock.
Who's there?
Dunce.
Dunce who?
Dunce say another word.

5

Will You Let Me In?

Knock, knock.
Who's there?
Earl.
Earl who?
Earl be glad to tell you if you open the door.

* * *

Knock, knock.
Who's there?
Ears.
Ears who?
Ears another knock-knock for you.

* * *

Knock, knock.
Who's there?
Eddie.
Eddie who?
Eddie body home?

★ ★ ★

Knock, knock.
Who's there?
Eggs.
Eggs who?
Eggstremely nice to meet you.

★ ★ ★

Knock, knock.
Who's there?
Elsie.
Elsie who?
Elsie you around.

★ ★ ★

Knock, knock.
Who's there?
Ember!
Ember who?
Ember me? I'm your best friend!

★ ★ ★

Knock, knock.
Who's there?
Emma.
Emma who?
Emma too early for lunch?

★ ★ ★

Knock, knock.
Who's there?
Europe.
Europe who?
Europe early this morning, can't you sleep?

★ ★ ★

Knock, knock.
Who's there?
European.
European who?
European in my bathroom and I need to use it!

★ ★ ★

Knock, knock.
Who's there?
Evans.
Evans who?
Evans to Betsy, you look tired!

★ ★ ★

Knock, knock.
Who's there?
Eye.
Eye who?
Eye know who you are. Don't you know who I am?

6

Am I at the Right House?

Knock, knock.
Who's there?
Falafel.
Falafel who?
Falafel my skateboard and landed on my knee.

★ ★ ★

Knock, knock.
Who's there?
Felipe.
Felipe who?
Felipe the bathtub–I need a wash.

★ ★ ★

Knock, knock.
Who's there?
I Felix.
I Felix who?
I Felix-cited.

★ ★ ★

Knock, knock.
Who's there?
Ferdie.
Ferdie who?
Ferdie last time, open the door!

★ ★ ★

Knock, knock.
Who's there?
Fido.
Fido who?
Fido known you were home, I'd have brought a cake.

★ ★ ★

Knock, knock.
Who's there?
Figs.
Figs who?
Figs the doorbell. It's been broken for ages!

★ ★ ★

Knock, knock.
Who's there?
Flea.
Flea who?
Flea blind mice.

★ ★ ★

Knock, knock.
Who's there?
Frankfurter.
Frankfurter who?
Frankfurter lovely evening.

★ ★ ★

Knock, knock.
Who's there?
Franz.
Franz who?
Franz, Romans, countrymen…

★ ★ ★

Knock, knock.
Who's there?
Fred.
Fred who?
Who's a Fred of the Big Bad Wolf?

★ ★ ★

Knock, knock.
Who's there?
Freddie.
Freddie who?
Freddie or not, here I come.

★ ★ ★

Knock, knock.
Who's there?
Freeze.
Freeze who?
Freeze a jolly good fellow.

★ ★ ★

Knock, knock.
Who's there?
Fresno.
Fresno who?
Rudolf the Fresno reindeer…

★ ★ ★

Knock, knock.
Who's there?
Furry.
Furry who?
Furry's a jolly good fellow.

7

Open Up!

Knock, knock.
Who's there?
Gandhi.
Gandhi who?
Gandhi you come out to play?

★ ★ ★

Knock, knock.
Who's there?
German border patrol.
German border patrol who?
Ve vill ask ze questions.

★ ★ ★

Knock, knock.
Who's there?
Gladys.
Gladys who?
Gladys summer, aren't you?

★ ★ ★

Knock, knock.
Who's there?
Gnats.
Gnats who?
Gnats not funny. Open up.

★ ★ ★

Knock, knock.
Who's there?
Goblin.
Goblin who?
Goblin food will make you sick.

★ ★ ★

Knock, knock.
Who's there?
Goliath.
Goliath who?
Goliath down. Thou lookest tired.

★ ★ ★

Knock, knock.
Who's there?
Gopher.
Gopher who?
Gopher a swim. It will refresh you.

★ ★ ★

Knock, knock.
Who's there?
Gorilla.
Gorilla who?
Gorilla cheese sandwiches are good with ketchup.

★ ★ ★

Knock, knock.
Who's there?
Grub.
Grub who?
Grub hold of my hand and let's go.

8

Anybody in There?

Knock, knock.
Who's there?
Hair combs.
Hair combs who?
Hair combs the bride!

★ ★ ★

Knock, knock.
Who's there?
Hairy.
Hairy who?
Hairy up, I haven't got all day!

★ ★ ★

Knock, knock.
Who's there?
Hank.
Hank who?
You're welcome.

★ ★ ★

Knock, knock.
Who's there?
Harp.
Harp who?
Harp the Herald Angels Sing!

★ ★ ★

Knock, knock.
Who's there?
Heart.
Heart who?
Heart to hear you. Talk louder.

★ ★ ★

Knock, knock.
Who's there?
Heavenly.
Heavenly who?
Heavenly met somewhere before?

★ ★ ★

Knock, knock.
Who's there?
Henrietta.
Henrietta who?
Henrietta grasshopper.

★ ★ ★

Knock, knock.
Who's there?
Hiram.
Hiram who?
Hiram fine–how are you?

★ ★ ★

Knock, knock.
Who's there?
Holmes.
Holmes who?
Holmes sweet home!

★ ★ ★

Knock, knock.
Who's there?
Hour.
Hour who?
I'm fine, thanks. How are you?

★ ★ ★

Knock, knock.
Who's there?
Howard.
Howard who?
Howard you like to come out with me?

★ ★ ★

Knock, knock.
Who's there?
Howell.
Howell who?
Howell I ever get in if you don't open the door?

★ ★ ★

Knock, knock.
Who's there?
Howl.
Howl who?
Howl you know who it is if you keep the door shut?

★ ★ ★

Knock, knock.
Who's there?
Hoyt.
Hoyt who?
Hoyt myself. Ouch!

★ ★ ★

Knock, knock.
Who's there?
Hugh.
Hugh who?
Hi there to you too.

9

I'll Get It!

Knock, knock.
Who's there?
Ice cream.
Ice cream who?
Ice cream as loudly as I can for ice cream.

★ ★ ★

Knock, knock.
Who's there?
Ida.
Ida who?
Ida written sooner, but I lost your address.

★ ★ ★

Knock, knock.
Who's there?
Ilona.
Ilona who?
Ilona Ranger.

★ ★ ★

Knock, knock.
Who's there?
Ina Claire.
Ina Claire who?
Ina Claire day you can see forever.

★ ★ ★

Knock, knock.
Who's there?
Iran.
Iran who?
Iran all the way here. Let me in.

★ ★ ★

Knock, knock.
Who's there?
Iran.
Iran who?
Iran all the way to third base.

★ ★ ★

Knock, knock.
Who's there?
Irish.
Irish who?
Irish I had a million dollars.

★ ★ ★

Knock, knock.
Who's there?
Irish.
Irish who?
Irish you a merry Christmas.

★ ★ ★

Knock, knock.
Who's there?
Irish.
Irish who?
Irish I knew the answers to this test.

★ ★ ★

Knock, knock.
Who's there?
Irish.
Irish who?
Irish you'd take me to the soccer game.

★ ★ ★

Knock, knock.
Who's there?
Isabel.
Isabel who?
Isabel out of order? I had to knock!

★ ★ ★

Knock, knock.
Who's there?
Isaiah!
Isaiah who?
Isaiah nothing else until you let me in.

★ ★ ★

Knock, knock.
Who's there?
Island.
Island who?
Island on my feet when I jump.

★ ★ ★

Knock, knock.
Who's there?
Ivor.
Ivor who?
Ivor sore hand from knocking at this door.

★ ★ ★

Knock, knock.
Who's there?
Izzy.
Izzy who?
Izzy come, izzy go.

★　★　★

Knock, knock.
Who's there?
Izzy.
Izzy who?
Izzy coming or isn't he?

10

Aren't You Going to Open the Door?

Knock, knock.
Who's there?
Jeff.
Jeff who?
Jeff in one ear. Please speak up.

★ ★ ★

Knock, knock.
Who's there?
Jerry.
Jerry who?
Jerry funny. You know who it is!

★ ★ ★

Knock, knock.
Who's there?
Jester.
Jester who?
Jester minute! I'm looking for my key!

★ ★ ★

Knock, knock.
Who's there?
Jester.
Jester who?
Jester silly old man.

★ ★ ★

Knock, knock.
Who's there?
Jethro.
Jethro who?
Jethro the key out of the window and I'll open the
    door.

★ ★ ★

Knock, knock.
Who's there?
Jewel.
Jewel who?
Jewel remember me after you see my face.

★ ★ ★

Knock, knock.
Who's there?
Jewel.
Jewel who?
Jewel do your homework if you know what's good
for you!

★ ★ ★

Knock, knock.
Who's there?
Joan.
Joan who?
Joan call us—we'll call you.

★ ★ ★

Knock, knock.
Who's there?
Juana.
Juana who?
Juana hear some more knock-knock jokes?

★ ★ ★

Knock, knock.
Who's there?
Juicy.
Juicy who?
Juicy who threw that snowball at me?

★ ★ ★

Knock, knock.
Who's there?
Justin.
Justin who?
Justin time for your dinner.

★ ★ ★

Knock, knock.
Who's there?
Justine.
Justine who?
Justine the nick of time.

11

Don't Knock So Loud!

Knock, knock.
Who's there?
Keanu.
Keanu who?
Keanu let me in? It's cold out here.

* * *

Knock, knock.
Who's there?
Ken.
Ken who?
Ken I come in? It's freezing out here!

* * *

Knock, knock.
Who's there?
Ken.
Ken who?
Ken you drive me to school? I missed the bus!

★ ★ ★

Knock, knock.
Who's there?
Kent.
Kent who?
Kent you tell who it is?

★ ★ ★

Knock, knock.
Who's there?
Kenya.
Kenya who?
Kenya give me a hand and open the door?

★ ★ ★

Knock, knock.
Who's there?
Kerry.
Kerry who?
Kerry me upstairs, would you? I'm pooped!

★ ★ ★

Knock, knock.
Who's there?
Ketchup.
Ketchup who?
Ketchup to her before she skates into that dumpster.

★ ★ ★

Knock, knock.
Who's there?
Kipper.
Kipper who?
Kipper hands to yourself.

★ ★ ★

Knock, knock.
Who's there?
Klaus.
Klaus who?
Klaus the window. I can hear your television all the
    way down the street!

★ ★ ★

Knock, knock.
Who's there?
Knoxville.
Knoxville who?
Knoxville always get your attention if I bang long
    enough.

12

Be Patient—
I'm Coming!

Knock, knock.
Who's there?
Larry.
Larry who?
Larry funny, now open the door.

★ ★ ★

Knock, knock.
Who's there?
Leggo.
Leggo who?
Leggo of me and I'll tell you!

★ ★ ★

Knock, knock.
Who's there?
Leif.
Leif who?
Leif me alone.

* * *

Knock, knock.
Who's there?
Les.
Les who?
Les go for a swim before we eat.

* * *

Knock, knock.
Who's there?
Letter.
Letter who?
Letter in or she'll knock the door down.

* * *

Knock, knock.
Who's there?
Lettuce.
Lettuce who?
Lettuce in, why don't you?

* * *

Knock, knock.
Who's there?
Lion.
Lion who?
Lion here on your doorstep. Open up.

★ ★ ★

Knock, knock.
Who's there?
Lionel.
Lionel who?
Lionel bite your hand if you stick it in the cage.

★ ★ ★

Knock, knock.
Who's there?
Lisa.
Lisa who?
Lisa you can do is let me in.

★ ★ ★

Knock, knock.
Who's there?
Little old lady.
Little old lady who?
I didn't know you could yodel.

★ ★ ★

Knock, knock.
Who's there?
Locker.
Locker who?
Locker in the closet if you find her!

★ ★ ★

Knock, knock.
Who's there?
Luck.
Luck who?
Luck through the keyhole.

★ ★ ★

Knock, knock.
Who's there?
Luke.
Luke who?
Luke snappy and open the door.

★ ★ ★

Knock, knock.
Who's there?
Luke.
Luke who?
Luke through the peephole and you'll see.

Knock, knock.
Who's there?
Luke.
Luke who?
Luke before you leap.

13

I Just Want to Visit!

Knock, knock.
Who's there?
Madge.
Madge who?
Madge-in my surprise, you're home!

★ ★ ★

Knock, knock.
Who's there?
Major.
Major who?
Major answer a knock-knock joke.

★ ★ ★

Knock, knock.
Who's there?
Major.
Major who?
Major open the door, didn't I?

⭐ ⭐ ⭐

Knock, knock.
Who's there?
Mandy.
Mandy who?
Mandy lifeboats. The ship's sinking!

⭐ ⭐ ⭐

Knock, knock.
Who's there?
Manny.
Manny who?
Manny are called, few are chosen.

⭐ ⭐ ⭐

Knock, knock.
Who's there?
Max.
Max who?
Max no difference, just open the door!

Knock, knock.
Who's there?
Mayonnaise.
Mayonnaise who?
Mayonnaise have seen the glory of the coming of
the Lord.

★ ★ ★

Knock, knock.
Who's there?
Mice.
Mice who?
Mice to make your acquaintance.

★ ★ ★

Knock, knock.
Who's there?
Mickey!
Mickey who?
Mickey is stuck in the lock.

★ ★ ★

Knock, knock.
Who's there?
Midas.
Midas who?
Midas well let me in.

★ ★ ★

Knock, knock.
Who's there?
Midas.
Midas who?
Midas well sit down and relax.

★ ★ ★

Knock, knock.
Who's there?
Miniature.
Miniature who?
Miniature open your mouth, you put your foot in it.

★ ★ ★

Knock, knock.
Who's there?
Mira.
Mira who?
Mira, Mira on the wall, who's the fairest of them all?

★ ★ ★

Knock, knock.
Who's there?
Moscow.
Moscow who?
Moscows moo, but this one seems very quiet!

★ ★ ★

Knock, knock.
Who's there?
Muffin.
Muffin who?
Muffin ventured, muffin gained.

★ ★ ★

Knock, knock.
Who's there?
Myron.
Myron who?
Myron around the park marathon made me tired.

14

The Doorbell Is Broken!

Knock, knock.
Who's there?
Nana.
Nana who?
Nana your business.

★ ★ ★

Knock, knock.
Who's there?
Noah.
Noah who?
Noah good place to eat?

★ ★ ★

Knock, knock.
Who's there?
Noah.
Noah who?
Noah fence, but I'm not going to tell you the answer.

★ ★ ★

Knock, knock.
Who's there?
Noah.
Noah who?
Noahbody knows…

★ ★ ★

Knock, knock.
Who's there?
Norma Lee.
Norma Lee who?
Norma Lee I don't go to the beach without my
    glasses.

★ ★ ★

Knock, knock.
Who's there?
Norma Lee.
Norma Lee who?
Norma Lee I have my key.

15

Come at Another Time!

Knock, knock.
Who's there?
Olive.
Olive who?
Olive these food jokes are pretty lousy.

★ ★ ★

Knock, knock.
Who's there?
Ollie.
Ollie who?
Ollie said was that I should come visit you.

★ ★ ★

Knock, knock.
Who's there?
Ollie.
Ollie who?
Ollie want for Christmas is my two front teeth.

★ ★ ★

Knock, knock.
Who's there?
Omar.
Omar who?
Omar darling Clementine.

★ ★ ★

Knock, knock.
Who's there?
Omar.
Omar who?
Omar goodness, I'm late for class!

★ ★ ★

Knock, knock.
Who's there?
Omelet.
Omelet who?
Omelet smarter than I look!

★ ★ ★

Knock, knock.
Who's there?
Ooze.
Ooze who?
Ooze in charge around here?

★ ★ ★

Knock, knock.
Who's there?
Ooze.
Ooze who?
Ooze going to change my diaper?

★ ★ ★

Knock, knock.
Who's there?
Ooze.
Ooze who?
Ooze that knocking at my door?

★ ★ ★

Knock, knock.
Who's there?
Osborn.
Osborn who?
Osborn today! That makes it my birthday!

★ ★ ★

Knock, knock.
Who's there?
Oscar.
Oscar who?
Oscar silly question, get a silly answer.

Knock, knock.
Who's there?
Owl.
Owl who?
Owl aboard.

Knock, knock.
Who's there?
Ox.
Ox who?
Ox me for a date and I may say yes.

16

I'm Tired of Waiting!

Knock, knock.
Who's there?
Pasture.
Pasture who?
Pasture bedtime, isn't it?

★ ★ ★

Knock, knock.
Who's there?
Patty O.
Patty O who?
Patty O'Furniture!

★ ★ ★

Knock, knock.
Who's there?
Paul.
Paul who?
Paul up a chair, and I'll tell you.

★ ★ ★

Knock, knock.
Who's there?
Peas.
Peas who?
Peas to meet you.

★ ★ ★

Knock, knock.
Who's there?
Pencil.
Pencil who?
Pencil fall down without a belt.

★ ★ ★

Knock, knock.
Who's there?
Phil.
Phil who?
Phil my drink for me, will you?

★ ★ ★

Knock, knock.
Who's there?
Police.
Police who?
Police let me in…it's raining out here!

★ ★ ★

Knock, knock.
Who's there?
Police.
Police who?
Police open the door.

★ ★ ★

Knock, knock.
Who's there?
Polly.
Polly who?
Polly wogs are just baby frogs.

★ ★ ★

Knock, knock.
Who's there?
Pucker.
Pucker who?
Pucker up, I'm gonna kiss you!

★ ★ ★

Knock, knock.
Who's there?
Punch.
Punch who?
Not me–I've just got here.

17

I Can't Come to the Door!

Knock, knock.
Who's there?
Quiche.
Quiche who?
Quiche me, you fool.

★ ★ ★

Knock, knock.
Who's there?
Radio.
Radio who?
Radio not, here I come.

★ ★ ★

Knock, knock.
Who's there?
Razor.
Razor who?
Razor your hands, this is a stick-up.

★ ★ ★

Knock, knock.
Who's there?
Red.
Red who?
Red pepper. Isn't that a hot one?

★ ★ ★

Knock, knock.
Who's there?
Rhoda.
Rhoda who?
Rhoda boat across da lake.

★ ★ ★

Knock, knock.
Who's there?
Rice.
Rice who?
Rice and shine, time to go to school.

★ ★ ★

Knock, knock.
Who's there?
Ripsaw.
Ripsaw who?
Ripsaw you downtown yesterday.

★ ★ ★

Knock, knock.
Who's there?
Rita.
Rita who?
Rita good book lately?

★ ★ ★

Knock, knock.
Who's there?
Roach.
Roach who?
Roach you a letter–why didn't you write back?

★ ★ ★

Knock, knock.
Who's there?
Robin.
Robin who?
Robin banks is what I do.

★ ★ ★

Knock, knock.
Who's there?
Robin.
Robin who?
Robin a coffin is dangerous. You could be in grave
  trouble.

★ ★ ★

Knock, knock.
Who's there?
Robot.
Robot who?
Robot don't splash with the oars.

★ ★ ★

Knock, knock.
Who's there?
Roland.
Roland who?
Roland butter taste good.

★ ★ ★

Knock, knock.
Who's there?
Ron.
Ron who?
Ron faster, there's a lion after us.

★ ★ ★

Knock, knock.
Who's there?
Roseanne.
Roseanne who?
Roseanne the tulip are my favorite flowers.

★ ★ ★

Knock, knock.
Who's there?
Roxanne.
Roxanne who?
Roxanne shells were scattered all over the beach.

★ ★ ★

Knock, knock.
Who's there?
Rufus.
Rufus who?
Rufus leaking. You'd better get it fixed.

18

Knock, Knock, Knock!

Knock, knock.
Who's there?
Saber.
Saber who?
Saber, she's drowning.

★ ★ ★

Knock, knock.
Who's there?
Sabina.
Sabina who?
Sabina long time since I last saw you.

★ ★ ★

Knock, knock.
Who's there?
Sacha.
Sacha who?
Sacha fuss, just because I knocked at your door.

* * *

Knock, knock.
Who's there?
Sacha.
Sacha who?
Sacha lot of questions in this exam.

* * *

Knock, knock.
Who's there?
Sadie.
Sadie who?
Sadie magic words, and I'll tell you.

* * *

Knock, knock.
Who's there?
Sahara.
Sahara who?
Sahara you today?

* * *

Knock, knock.
Who's there?
Salmon.
Salmon who?
Salmon Jack are over at my house.

★ ★ ★

Knock, knock.
Who's there?
Sam.
Sam who?
Sam day, you'll remember.

★ ★ ★

Knock, knock.
Who's there?
Samoa.
Samoa who?
Samoa knock-knock jokes.

★ ★ ★

Knock, knock.
Who's there?
Sandy.
Sandy who?
Sandy Claus!

★ ★ ★

Knock, knock.
Who's there?
Santa Anna.
Santa Anna who?
Santa Anna gonna bring you anything if you don't
believe in him.

★ ★ ★

Knock, knock.
Who's there?
Sarah.
Sarah who?
Sarah doctor in the house?

★ ★ ★

Knock, knock.
Who's there?
Scold.
Scold who?
Scold outside. Please let me in.

★ ★ ★

Knock, knock.
Who's there?
Scold.
Scold who?
Scold enough to go ice-skating.

* * *

Knock, knock.
Who's there?
Senior.
Senior who?
Senior so nosy, I'm not going to tell you who it is!

* * *

Knock, knock.
Who's there?
Senior.
Senior who?
Senior uncle lately?

* * *

Knock, knock.
Who's there?
Senior.
Senior who?
Senior hockey stick around here lately?

* * *

Knock, knock.
Who's there?
Seymour.
Seymour who?
Seymour kittens out here?

★ ★ ★

Knock, knock.
Who's there?
Sharon.
Sharon who?
Sharon share alike.

★ ★ ★

Knock, knock.
Who's there?
Shelby.
Shelby who?
Shelby coming 'round the mountain when she comes.

★ ★ ★

Knock, knock.
Who's there?
Sherwood.
Sherwood who?
Sherwood like it if you'd let me kiss you.

★ ★ ★

Knock, knock.
Who's there?
Sherwood.
Sherwood who?
Sherwood like for you to let me in.

★ ★ ★

Knock, knock.
Who's there?
Sherwood.
Sherwood who?
Sherwood like to hear another knock-knock joke.

★ ★ ★

Knock, knock.
Who's there?
Shirley.
Shirley who?
Shirley you must be joking.

★ ★ ★

Knock, knock.
Who's there?
Sicily.
Sicily who?
Sicily question.

★ ★ ★

Knock, knock.
Who's there?
Snow.
Snow who?
Snow use. I've forgotten the name.

★ ★ ★

Knock, knock.
Who's there?
Socket.
Socket who?
Socket to me!

★ ★ ★

Knock, knock.
Who's there?
Soda.
Soda who?
Soda you like me?

★ ★ ★

Knock, knock.
Who's there?
Sofa.
Sofa who?
Sofa you're doing fine.

★ ★ ★

Knock, knock.
Who's there?
Sofa.
Sofa who?
Sofa so good!

★ ★ ★

Knock, knock.
Who's there?
Somber.
Somber who?
Somber over the rainbow.

★ ★ ★

Knock, knock.
Who's there?
Specter.
Specter who?
Specter Holmes of Scotland Yard.

★ ★ ★

Knock, knock.
Who's there?
Spell.
Spell who?
W-H-O!

★ ★ ★

Knock, knock.
Who's there?
Spinach.
Spinach who?
Spinaching me so long I had to scratch it.

★ ★ ★

Knock, knock.
Who's there?
Stan.
Stan who?
Stan aside–I'm coming through.

★ ★ ★

Knock, knock.
Who's there?
Stella.
Stella who?
Stella nother crazy knock-knock joke.

★ ★ ★

Knock, knock.
Who's there?
Stopwatch.
Stopwatch who?
Stopwatch you're doing this minute.

★ ★ ★

Knock, knock.
Who's there?
Stu.
Stu who?
Stu late to ask questions.

★ ★ ★

Knock, knock.
Who's there?
Sue.
Sue who?
Sue prize.

★ ★ ★

Knock, knock.
Who's there?
Sultan.
Sultan who?
Sultan pepper.

★ ★ ★

Knock, knock.
Who's there?
Sultan.
Sultan who?
Sultan pepper makes everything taste better!

★ ★ ★

Knock, knock.
Who's there?
Sum Toi.
Sum Toi who?
Sum Toi you've got there.

★ ★ ★

Knock, knock.
Who's there?
Summertime.
Summertime who?
Summertime itsa hot, summertime itsa cold.

★ ★ ★

Knock, knock.
Who's there?
Summertime.
Summertime who?
Summertime I'm going to stop telling knock-knock
    jokes.

★ ★ ★

Knock, knock.
Who's there?
Sushi.
Sushi who?
Sushi told me to look you up!

★ ★ ★

Knock, knock.
Who's there?
Swarm.
Swarm who?
Swarm enough to go swimming.

★ ★ ★

Knock, knock.
Who's there?
Sweden.
Sweden who?
Sweden my lemonade with some sugar, will you?

★ ★ ★

Knock, knock.
Who's there?
Sweden.
Sweden who?
Sweden my tea with two lumps of sugar, please.

19

Too Much Knocking!

Knock, knock.
Who's there?
Taffilda.
Taffilda who?
Taffilda bucket you have to turn on the water.

★ ★ ★

Knock, knock.
Who's there?
Tamara.
Tamara who?
Tamara it's gonna rain.

★ ★ ★

Knock, knock.
Who's there?
Tamara.
Tamara who?
Tamara I have an important meeting.

⭐ ⭐ ⭐

Knock, knock.
Who's there?
Tara.
Tara who?
Tara-ra-boom-de-ay!

⭐ ⭐ ⭐

Knock, knock.
Who's there?
Tarzan.
Tarzan who?
Tarzan stripes forever.

⭐ ⭐ ⭐

Knock, knock.
Who's there?
Telly.
Telly who?
Telly Phone.

⭐ ⭐ ⭐

Knock, knock.
Who's there?
Thatcher.
Thatcher who?
Thatcher was a funny joke.

 ★ ★ ★

Knock, knock.
Who's there?
Thea.
Thea who?
Thea later, alligator.

★ ★ ★

Knock, knock.
Who's there?
Theodore.
Theodore who?
Theodore is closed. Open up!

★ ★ ★

Knock, knock.
Who's there?
Theophilus.
Theophilus who?
Theophilus storm I've ever seen out here!

★ ★ ★

Knock, knock.
Who's there?
Theresa.
Theresa who?
Theresa fly in my soup.

★ ★ ★

Knock, knock.
Who's there?
Thermos.
Thermos who?
Thermos be a better knock-knock than this one.

★ ★ ★

Knock, knock.
Who's there?
Thermos.
Thermos who?
Thermos be someone home, I hear the radio
    playing.

★ ★ ★

Knock, knock.
Who's there?
Thermos.
Thermos who?
Thermos be someone waiting who feels the way I
    do.

★ ★ ★

Knock, knock.
Who's there?
Thesis.
Thesis who?
Thesis a stickup!

★ ★ ★

Knock, knock.
Who's there?
Thistle.
Thistle who?
Thistle be a lesson to me.

★ ★ ★

Knock, knock.
Who's there?
Thistle.
Thistle who?
Thistle make you whistle.

★ ★ ★

Knock, knock.
Who's there?
Thumb.
Thumb who?
Thumb like it hot, thumb like it cold.

* * *

Knock, knock.
Who's there?
Thumping.
Thumping who?
Thumping green and slimy just went up your trousers.

* * *

Knock, knock.
Who's there?
Tic tac.
Tic tac who?
Tic tac paddy whack, give the dog a bone.

* * *

Knock, knock.
Who's there?
Tomb.
Tomb who?
Tomb whom it may concern!

* * *

Knock, knock.
Who's there?
Torch.
Torch who?
Torch you would never ask.

20

All Right, All Right— I'm Coming!

Knock, knock.
Who's there?
Unawares.
Unawares who?
Unawares what you put on first every morning.

★ ★ ★

Knock, knock.
Who's there?
Upton.
Upton who?
Upton now it's been pretty quiet around here.

★ ★ ★

Knock, knock.
Who's there?
Venice.
Venice who?
Venice your birthday?

★ ★ ★

Knock, knock.
Who's there?
Vera.
Vera who?
Vera interesting.

★ ★ ★

Knock, knock.
Who's there?
A vet.
A vet who?
A vet ya vant to let me in.

★ ★ ★

Knock, knock.
Who's there?
Wade.
Wade who?
Wade till I get inside, then I'll tell you!

★ ★ ★

Knock, knock.
Who's there?
Warrant.
Warrant who?
Warrant you home before?

★ ★ ★

Knock, knock.
Who's there?
Warrior.
Warrior who?
Warrior been all my life?

★ ★ ★

Knock, knock.
Who's there?
Yah.
Yah who?
I didn't know you were a cowboy.

★ ★ ★

Knock, knock.
Who's there?
Zombies.
Zombies who?
Zombies make honey, and zombies just buzz around.

Other Books by Bob Phillips

All-Time Awesome Collection
of Good Clean Jokes for Kids

The Awesome Book
of Bible Trivia

The Awesome Book
of Heavenly Humor

Awesome Good Clean
Jokes for Kids

Awesome Knock-Knock
Jokes for Kids

The Best of the Good
Clean Jokes

Dude, Got Another Joke?

Extremely Good Clean
Jokes for Kids

Fabulous and Funny
Clean Jokes for Kids

Good Clean Jokes to Drive
Your Parents Crazy

Good Clean Knock-Knock
Jokes for Kids

How Can I Be Sure?

How to Deal with
Annoying People

Jolly Jokes for Older Folks

Laughter from
the Pearly Gates

Over the Hill & On a Roll

Over the Next Hill
& Still Rolling

Over the Top Clean
Jokes for Kids

Overcoming Anxiety
and Depression

Super Incredible Knock-Knock
Jokes for Kids

The World's Greatest
Collection of Clean Jokes

The World's Greatest
Knock-Knock Jokes for Kids

For more information, send a self-addressed
stamped envelope to:

Family Services
P.O. Box 9363
Fresno, California 93702